MAD
FOR
MEAT

KEVIN SIMMONDS

salmonpoetry

Published in 2011 by
Salmon Poetry
Cliffs of Moher, County Clare, Ireland
Website: www.salmonpoetry.com
Email: info@salmonpoetry.com

ISBN 978-1-907056-82-6

COVER IMAGE & COVER DESIGN: *Nori Hara – www.norihara.com*
TYPESETTING: *Siobhán Hutson*

PRINTED IN IRELAND

To four who finished here and now know the answers to
every single mystery:

Anthony Edwards, friend and mentor
Mitchell McCarthy, beloved cousin and dancer
Carrie Allen McCray-Nickens, friend and teacher
Trina Schexnider, darling aunt, artist and writer

Acknowledgements

Acknowledgements are due to the editors of the following in which some of the poems from this collection first appeared:

42opus
The American Poetry Journal
Anti-
Callaloo: A Journal of African Diaspora Arts and Letters
Cave Canem 10 X 10 Anthology
Chroma: A Queer Literary Journal
Coon Bidness
The Drunken Boat
FIELD Magazine
Ganymede Unfinished
Gathering Ground: A Reader Celebrating Cave Canem's First Decade
Jack Straw Writers Anthology
jubilat
Kyoto Journal
Main Street Rag
Nimrod
PANK Magazine
Poetry
REM Magazine
RHINO Poetry
The Ringing Ear: Black Poets Lean South
Rock & Sling
Salt Hill
storySouth
To Be Left With the Body
Typecast
War Diaries
WarpLand: A Journal of Black Literature and Ideas

Contents

Gift

He saw a galaxy
in meat

& from all over
they brought their cuts

laid them down
for him to divine

iridescent foil or the way
it locked into bone

No one knows
. . .

But he saw car brakes
jam

unresponsive as lungs
in a grandson's chest

as the inhaler lies
miles away

on the bathroom sink
. . .

& there were the winning numbers
shining from a mutton shank

Once   he bent down
left ear listening

to a loin
as if through a trapdoor

The poor
or misinformed

would bring turnips
or misshapen potatoes

He tried with those
& gills of fish

but could never find
the pulse

Certainty

Without traveling to Nashville
I still know that a boy there falls
piecemeal
into women's clothes
that in New Orleans
those overtaken by the water
rose inside
that water

Jehovah smells of mint?
Allah of gunpowder?

No

Even I recognize love failing
in ways it must

Plots

Fundamentalists have tracts
tiny plots of folded paper

gripped by salvation
bolted to truth

Tracts are plots too narrow
for living men

Bolt from anyone
gripping one

moseying toward you smiling salvation
ailing with truth

Sermon

It's too simple for most. Our cellular bodies are prosthetic to spirit, irrefutable elision of god and monster, wing and hangnail.

We are four-limbed embers.

Mostly it's recovery. Take the cliché of a child whose need for an absent father unearths an appetite for damage. This is the beginning of the gospel.

Before he had hair on his balls, he'd pled for deliverance. Some clapboard apostle shouted the demon names of what afflicts while that boy coughed into brown paper bags to expel his homosexuality. He retched until his stomach and sides ached.

The prayer should not always begin *Our Father.*

Not every two bodies will create children. It's not that they are without string, key or hammer. Some are woodwinds, their music of erotic conclusions. Let the breath pass through them. You do not control the wind.

The body doesn't know religion but begins its every motion as a god.

Saigon

He masturbates me under
a clean white towel
I've come for the metaphor
above the entrance

   Golden Smile

And isn't this why
we fought in Vietnam

the commerce between us
baby oil unifying skins
the opal of us shimmering
before my shot of silver   later
the shower's steam thick
among locals and foreigners
satisfied with such extravagance
for so cheap

The dollar is strong
Currency of the weak

Abduction

That my mother claims she saw a UFO while waiting at the bus stop
is not what worries me. It's her waiting with the TV on
since that childhood sighting. She expects some sign.
A wink inside the late night infomercial. Then return.

If I had syringe-long fingers. If I shimmered instead of spoke.
If my filament glowed in the dark and blackness pooled in my irises.
Maybe then she'd look at me, smile and say,
I knew you'd come.

bouquet of scalpels

give the wound   finally
a mouth
a smile on each wrist

come rot with me

or trembling
withstand memory

who will claim me
that day
toe-tagged
& childless
never returned to the south
& its perfected agonies
nearly 40
still with every candle
ever lit
& blown out in me
a father unforgivably christian
& Jamaican
fine without my call
on father's day

sure-handed

i could castrate him
he who led me to doubt
black men could love

observe him without seed
his rightful & clean erection
observe as meat falls

there would be no lesson in that

instead
i take cover
in another man's body
as he takes cover
in mine

Basketball

I've played only once
which is unnatural really
the lesson in it
being so natural

For when you're caught and can't
make it
you look for an open man
to pass your load

With just a ball as excuse
I could join the machine
feeding a bottomless vowel
and dangling from it
the only net I know
made to let go

Emissary

Trip the wire
open your fist
wrap every finger around the throat
of the word

    Faggot is a shovel

Step onto the ledge of your body

    Faggot is a pearl

Steep in the hot water
of everybody else's
say so

    Faggot is a destiny

Spread your mocha no
your mocha mind your business
your mocha fuck you

    Faggot is a verb

Turn the hot water of that
into something you can swallow

Little Dolly Parton

saw the town trollop
as the goddess she wanted to be
despite what everyone said
about that scandal
in a too tight dress
blush slashed face
birds nest hair and a crossing of the street
that took every eye with her

I saw men I wanted to be

The goateed drama teacher
in grade school
loose cowboy booted stride
straight ruler of his attention
and me measuring up
as I recited Langston Hughes

The Jeri curled choir director
a gospel triad at the ready
in his throat   foot heavy
on the organ pedals

The Jesuit priest at Corpus Christi
who wore the brightest vestments
on holy days and lifted the host
as I rang the bells in my white robe
altar boy full of shame

Dolly what happened in the one room cabin
in Locust Ridge
How did you know it was love enough
for a cinched waist and blond wig
an altar of pentecostal breasts
and their rising hallelujah
at every breath

Tenor

He's baby faced
so those who want to father
first look there
even with the grey flecks at his temples
to his smallish mouth

And it's no exaggeration
to say his eyes
open for assurances
he'll be made to obey
be held steady by the promise
in a man's nonchalance

whatever he wants a father to be
reward for years of forced imagination
how a man would hold him with innocence
of the blood between them

Left to wonder
he imagines how
to build a father
A father needs to be seduced
at the urinals
sure you'll swallow
after the fuck
even the shit on the tip

The baby faced man is a singer
and when I listen to his voice
I'm unconvinced the trembling vibrato
is really his
But it is a voice

Something Owed

The man across the street
would undo his trousers
and ask me to squeeze lotion
into his underpants
He never touched me
only himself

Some days   it's sudden
Some days   it comes on slow

    the unbuckling   the scent of aloe and musk
    fingers serenading
    beneath herringbone trousers   later
    momma telling me how nice it is
    him taking to me so

Among men
how many give a daily recital
such as this
somewhere in memory

Anti-

Starts with the gel cap, then oozing from its soluble cell, time-released harnesses. The head pulling, pulled into a ladder. Each revolver slowly lifts its blues. No press conferences. Play dates, finally & wormholes. Anything for art.

Upon Hearing Leontyne Price on the United Negro College Fund Commercial

I ignored the boys who called me sissy
sang loudly in an operatic voice all the commercials
the theme from *Good Times*
Donna Summer too
But my spine lengthened the night I heard you open
the black fan of your voice
on primetime
Turbaned goddess of my Zenith
the way God struck your soprano
how you rang
We're not asking for a handout, just a hand!

Bad Catholics

Results from a McGill University study, released yesterday, suggest that people — men, anyways — become less aggressive at the sight of meat.

— *The Montreal Gazette*

We kept the butcher's block bloody
through Lent

Calm coming over us like gravy
at the sight of pot roast

A stew of slowed cognition
we were blunt in our surrender

Five boys & a husband
mom knew to do this decades ago

& kept an eye on the butcher
his tender wrists & special discounts

whenever dad made the trip alone
to bring home the lamb

swaddled in white paper
& marked

Sighted

Nature poet handling his plume
Urban poet   his switchblade

Each with wings unfolding in their hands

One travels the boned corset of cactus
sky lifting its hoop skirt to a meringue of stars

The other eulogizes children fallen from loveliness   filed
into caskets

Both behold faces turning to see
and be seen

They scatter the broken mirror everywhere

twang

grown woman
my momma
but winces
every time
she hears it

    tobacco wet baritone
    last thing you hear
    before nodding off
    long necked
    from a country oak

    slingshot nasal lingering
    on the *n* of *nigger*
    & *never*

momma has good ears
listening for the night riders
who ride across memory

i could never know it all
but the tight strings of a banjo
might cause her
to throw back her head
call out for me
to come

a sentence

needs
at least one subject
and one verb
(though sometimes the subject
is unnamed   it's understood

nevertheless
objects must be named)

    Johannes Mehserle shot Oscar Grant III.

subject: Johannes Mehserle
verb: shot
object: Oscar Grant III

a sentence becomes sophisticated
when it includes complexity and detail

    Johannes Mehserle shot Oscar Grant III who was restrained faced down
    on the ground surrounded by three police officers.

subject: Johannes Mehserle
verb: shot
object: Oscar Grant III

    A white police officer shot a black man faced down on the ground
    and will spend less than two years in jail for his criminal conviction.

what is the object
of that sentence?

object? anyone?

Cud

Whatever wonder there is to wake Saturday morning
and with my father pass the spade to weed between bricks
turn soil in beds

Whatever wonder there is to receive a letter from my mother
her longhand opposing distances

Whatever wonder there is   I've imagined

Not all of us are fatally vacant

Our mistakes mouthwatering   rich
in regret
daily allowances to break
down swallow keep
down

Enzymes enough in us to grow a field   some
thousand fields

Cord

If mother appears as a bruise
across your righting arm

sensitive even to the weight
of a silk sleeve

then you are her most human child
skin starring into coverlet

nothing less than kindling
for cover

You stare attuned
to that jagged injury

your tissue
exposed for puncture

with something like a screw or its driver
& without any force stronger than a slip

a mistake
a habit

Geography

I'm at a bar slash Middle Eastern novelty store slash coffee house in northern Japan. Tsuyoshi, the bartender, is quiet. Together, we fit no stereotype. We're alone. An African statue leans against the wall (a woman with breasts like bananas, a small drum in her belly). Ice melts as Lady Day simmers overhead.

Tsuyoshi's drying glasses and wondering about me, why I would bring my body all this way and sit across from him and the glasses he's setting down like chess pieces. He's wondering why I'd come to live in a small town only to be misunderstood: the language gathering in my throat like the sound of dead beetles crunching underfoot.

Hip Hop Nation

Japanese girls torment me
With chirpy unfortunate English

they *ask*
From America

Hip hop very like
My body is news of their arrival

They've landed in America   they're sure
because the static across my body has cleared

and I'm blacker than they'd imagined
I hardly look at them

Other black men run
into the tendrils of their gardens

They don't see Medusa's helmet there
tossed and eaten through

Enka

Her kimono-swollen glide
to center stage fluorescent
was the burning wick

Takes me back
Magic carpeted to the 70s
soundtracks swollen with brass
like in *Hawaii Five-O*
Give me the quiver of vibrato
swaying hips as it strikes
Give me the kimonoed diva
milking the interlude
staring into the distance
and taking us with her
Let me applaud
the obligatory applause
after the first chorus
pressed into my seat
by sequined despair   a throat filled
with pink flamingos

Represent

I can tell by your face that you're looking for bass.
— Samantha Raheem Thornhill

Bass insinuating itself
from a souped-up Honda
Two Japanese dudes heavy
in their front-seat recline
Surprised to see me
they giggle like the girls
they've just become
and bob tanned faces
like doorknockers
I answer with a smile and something
in flawless Japanese
I'm the black sensei
that hip hop folk singer standing
in the shelter of a bass line
six thousand miles from home

Scribbled on the Dust Jacket of My Favorite Book of Haiku

Winter, 2001 — Tono City, Japan

Manholes never relent in the white spillage
They issue forth like sores on a pale woman
like pennies tossed from God's warmest hands

Color Me

He cruised me across from Holiday Inn
junior year
thought my body mouthwatering
as he straddled me in the dorm bed
unbuttoning my pants
joyous to find it already hard and wet

Your black body is so beautiful
God I want you

Thunder in his mouth
Yet the most delicate music swells with restraint

God knows there's a *Have mercy*
just below my Adam's apple
when I've gotten an Asian man
into my hands
but I don't say

Your tiny waist
hooded bite-size purple-vaulted dick
Your willingness to let me beat
the drum of you

I don't *say* that
I just beat the drum

Singapore

We weren't drunk
He lifted his arms
in knowing surrender
T shirt first
then my hands steady
on his shorts   a slow
embrace down thighs calves
pooling at his feet

His silence was duty
The eclipse
this pleading

   Overtake me

Two years ago and now
he's graduated university
in love with a woman
who knows my name
seen my face in pictures
but can't know (how could she)
that I wish her dead and me
there ready to console

Whatever's vicious in this
has to be
Have you seen the violence
of the natural world
Thick paws stamping out
a path
to what's desired
needs first to be captured   rescued

Apple Tree

If today is the day I become a man
today I will grow taller than my father
and my voice will descend
slow to deliberateness
I will settle on a way and finally understand
the apple tree

   crouched down as if something brutal had happened
   for the sweetness to come

Rosebud

At Babylon
I fingered a Thai regular
He had English enough
to tell me his dreams
And if you know how a Thai boy
can make you remember years from that moment
even the faint rising music of his voice
you know if what I remember most
is how much flesh pouted from his hole —
what's left
of the force taken
to make him feel named
to tighten
to swell
to arrive at such supple
virtuosity —
then you know our own bodies
aren't the only lessons
we're given

the singing

allow some
to fall away
let it fall
twin to dust
what we are
twin to water
what is meant
to fall away
let's consent
to fall away
twin to dust
twin to gold
human lord
not far away
let it fall
closer still
what we are
what is meant
to fall away
everywhere
is closer still
everywhere
to fall away
human lord
twin to gold
twin to dust
allow some
closer still
to fall away
allow some
from far away
let them fall
to who we are
human lord

what we are
twin to gold
what we are
closer still
twins we are

salt (a suicide meditation)

my mother stepped into the sea
somewhere else

so we didn't see this
same sea held us

had us after we'd
given the voices all

verse & chorus
of all we'd fleshed

& withstood
until we thought

we could
no longer

my friend Jaya was there
his cinnamon stalk body

swaying in status
three letters sounding

as if the body might as well
give itself up

finally
to the water

there's reason
there's salt

& such span
you'd never know

who else is there
stung & possessed

by loss
its promises

its required letting
go

& this is a hard
poetic turn

but there is singing
deep from the floor

through phosphorescence
of magnified quadrillion atoms

each armed to beget ceaselessly
& unceasingly ring

their small bell bodies
into our belled bodies

& we & we
& we & we

&we &we
&we

NOTE: opening lines taken from *You Try
and Hope You're Wrong* by Blas Falconer

July in St. Helena

vine workers pass like *la brisa calma*
though my windows
as i ease up on the gas to San Francisco
an hour away
one dirty white man against a newspaper rack
by Walgreens waiting
for anyone to look
i will but won't say *sorry*
i don't have a job either
& poetry doesn't change that
the slant of *sorry*
doesn't ease his tightened throat
when the vine worker hears
there are five too many & he
may be one of them
saying in his mind
mi hija mi hija
like Hail Mary without the beads
now dangling from his rear view
what is want   what is need
what's sweat without the breeze
my stepfather would say
in his wide brimmed hat staring
at how delicate i would always be
how scared he was of that

Corrective Rape

Sizakele oh
& Salome

Eudy oh
your feet

stabbed your soles
like that

where your walking be
where your traveling be

whatever can be done on earth
will be done

just think of you to know I
& know I

must see
with every eye

they dug in you

The Poet, 1955

After poor Emmett Till
he wrote a poem to work out his faith
in things unseen

We'd all seen too much
    Emmett's water-logged face the teenage in him
    snatched by his opened mouth to a dog of a woman

    a mother seeing what the South
    had conjured for her son
    and the radiance of her voice

    in front of the cameras
    full rising
    through the falling

    of her son
Sunday following
Reverend had him recite

He called Emmett Till a mansion
a mansion of a boy
whose rooms we must fill

Book Lover's Minutes

July 4, 1946, Charleston

We opened with the Club song, followed by the Lord's Prayer.
The minutes were read and we dealt with all at hand: the Club
tea, Wright and his *Black Boy*, alms to the poor, and the Urban
League's request that all Negroes stay away from the State Fair.
Negroes are appointed to one particular day. We closed with a
vote to stay away, withhold our money, and shake our heads.
I've cried for this, for my grandson, for the lost giggles in the
House of Mirrors, the held breath on the Ferris wheel, for the
cotton candy I would have wiped from his cheeks.

Charleston Inferno

Had the tattlers not tattled
even babies

would've been pinned under flames
white skin dancing apart to the jig

> *Sins of the father*
> *make this right*

But the tattlers did tattle
and Strom's kind

had a line

Denmark knew

spare an orphan or faithful
Negroes

their tongues and dicks are bound
to whittle vendettas

They tried Vesey
I've tried him too

His testament   the slipped halo
round his throat

Aunt Jemima

My momma put a scarf 'round my head when I was a child. I can't hardly remember my head without it. It don't even come off no more. I dream of combs, of a man undoing the knot, taking me away somewhere.

I comfort. Sticky sweet maple flow of bosom they been sucking since 1889. Uncle Ben know what I'm talking 'bout. We comfort.

Flat worlds stacked one on top the other. I holds them together.

Never mind that update they say they did 20 years ago, when they replaced my scarf and gave me pearls and a lace collar. That ain't me.

Tell me something sweet, something that'll stick and undo the knots I known.

Eartha Kitt

I was born Eartha Mae in a state with "south" in its name —
the one where there was cotton to run from. When I was eight
years old my mother sent me to New York to live with my
aunt. No one would take her in with a half-white child.

I'll spare you the chronology but I know the distance between
dirt and diamonds. Darling, I've traveled it.

Ladybird Johnson asked what I thought of the war and I told
her — *in* the White House.

I was blacklisted. Europe took me into her bosom as she's done
for black artists over the century. Paul Robeson, Katherine
Dunham, Sidney Bechet, Oliver Harrington. Eartha Kitt.

Bayard Rustin

The Movement. That's what I work for. The March on Washington for Jobs and Freedom. It's going to make an impact.

I served 60 days in Pasadena for "sex perversion." There's a hush around that. People in and outside of the Movement have threatened to make a story out of me. Right now, there are more necessary stories.

The rights I don't possess because I'm a Negro certainly come before those I yearn for as a homosexual. Homosexual. Such an antiseptic sound to it. Yet I rather that to other names, names I'm called between teeth.

There isn't time to be disgusted with me. Everyone must be disgusted with rights willfully and criminally delayed.

In Praise of the New York Stenographer who Disrespected Paul Robeson

Had she not given voice to the Klan
within

his steel-eyed voice might have remained
on that island

thinning democratically
in the courtroom

I never take dictation from a nigger
Operatic

She was nourishment enough
to leave the Bar

Deliverance

for Paul Robeson

Big black booming bloom
a man
fanning the blistering rod
His voice and us still passing through
the opened sea

After Katrina

There's no Sabbath in this house
Just work

The black of garbage bags
yellow-cinched throats opening
to gloved hands

Black tombs along the road now
proof she knew to cherish
the passing things

even those muted before the water came
before the mold's grotesquerie
and the wooden house choked on bones

My aunt wades through the wreckage   failing
no matter how hard she tries
at letting go

I look on glad at her failing
her slow rites
fingering what she'd once been given to care for

The waistbands of her husband's briefs
elastic as memory
the blank stare of rotted drawers

their irises of folded linen still
smelling of soap and wood
and clean hands

Daylight through these silent windows
and I'm sure now   Today is Sabbath
the work we do   prayer

I know what she releases into the garbage bags
shiny like wet skins of seals
beached on the shore of this house

Crude

H2
its smothered
O

circling
for sense

there is none

three-eyed
or blind

delirious
with repair

eventually
or now

Folktale of the Skinny Elephant

after the elephant carving
(Dr. Joseph Al Towles Archival Collection, Avery Center)

I ate a white man and this is what happened to my body
I ate a white man because he wanted the white flowers
on my face I ate the white man who wanted
the flowers on my face because
my face is Africa I ate
the white man because
he came to Africa
to cut back the
) overgrowth (
) the body (
) crowded (
) with bones (
) the body (
crowded
with
bones
with
bones
with
bones

Witchcraft

A woman came out of me
Black and undisturbed
A redheaded boy child
Pale as a potato chip
A Chinese man
Lips pink as an eardrum
Open eyed Indian child
Her face framed with flies
The corners of her mouth
Crusted over with hunger
A Jew bobbing his head in supplication
His ringlets like my mother's

One a moth-faced child
One a deliverer
One a sex offender
One who screamed from the hospital bed parked
In the living room
One who remembered the black of her father's belt
One who is armed to forget
One who had a fetus taken from her womb
Purple and destroyed

A woman came out of me
Black and undisturbed

how the living

with white crests bordering
each cuticle

cast higher
on either thumb

even with that light
folded into your darkroom body

so long practiced in fracture   you
conceive a fumbling

white egged
headstrong

before the eyes settle
you bleat

hands cupped
ovals like feeders

speechless & shoveled
you are wood bent wet

. . .
. . .

before your ashes
measure against regret

that family-sized regret
toted from childhood

to your house warm with coffee
& nightclothes

as you settle in bed
copper to his hammer   to hers

a Buddhist thing will happen
in the mouth layer

your fingers for Chopin
soldier on in music

An Old Man Carrying His Catheter Bag

white-haired vapor
in khakis
shuffling down a street

held it waist high
a flag
signaling the body

solid   liquid   gas
the body comes
to all three

I am bile
as I am wit
I drink to live in this body

See to it that you revere
this gold
this gold

Inheritance

My mother dies overweight
legs tight
with fluid
a rash crusted
beneath her socks
my Mississippi stepfather
on his oxygen machine
playing the lottery
toothless but with gums
that crack nuts
clean rib bones
forget what once
stood sharp
& tore meat
chewed rice my mother cooked
to tender
bit
his tongue
before he called me
faggot
Soon mama will bequeath
this slow drip that dulls
remembering
leave me toothless
mad
for meat

Tornado

We huddled in the fallout beneath the house like we'd done each time before. My brother and me. The bass droned long enough for him to unbutton my jeans. His hands felt better than mine ever had. And though I couldn't see his face to know anything for sure, I bet his lazy eye would no longer be his greatest shame. The greater shifting was this side the latch.

While others went up to see what was left, we stayed below, holding hands like brothers sometimes do when danger's come and gone and you stand there together betting how long it'll take for the rushing blackness to drop from sight and leave you to wander this side the wreckage.

San Francisco (op. 11)

lesbians all around
in varying degrees of welcome & lamentation

we are didactic but not all
vegan green & slow food

chestnut st. saturated
with nail parlors

paraffin wax enough to be smooth
as asians

at post & larkin
perfumed & bosomed

tranny be thy names
one eyeing me

not like a gambler
at his wedding ring

but like an altar boy who's discovered
his relevance & will accelerate his body

high-minded & worried
we attend well-lit poetry readings

& art exhibits
independent houses we hear about

on facebook
we are disgusted

with diminishing black bodies
& the gym's increasing fee

our teeth are whitened
while the compost fills

we are septic & dissatisfied
with our attention spans

yet there will never be less
than there is now

we have not enough parking spaces
as chinatown remains chinese

clothes hanging from windows
above fading characters

& like everywhere
delivery matters in san francisco

when the korean grocer on fillmore ruins
my day with insinuation

& not a word passes between us
only a price

then I unwrap the gum to chew through
hurt & anger

swallow the flavors of
hollywood & oakland

without a white lover
or some other neutralizing companion

to take away my strut
& pointed barrels

welcome to san francisco

send the visitors out
so we may know them

Feed

Every year, Nathan's Famous July Fourth International Hot Dog Eating Contest gives me an opportunity to see Takeru Kobayashi who is sexy. My aunt says Nathan's Famous July Fourth International Hot Dog Eating Contest is an outright sin. Add Nathan's Famous July Fourth International Hot Dog Eating Contest to a long list of embarrassing annual American events. What would Kobayashi do if a busload of starving children showed up at Nathan's Famous July Fourth International Hot Dog Eating Contest? I wonder what bulimics think of Nathan's Famous July Fourth International Hot Dog Eating Contest. The winning contestant at Nathan's Famous July Fourth International Hot Dog Eating Contest usually consumes upwards of 20,000 calories. Nathan's Famous July Fourth International Hot Dog Eating Contest, *tsk tsk tsk*. I wouldn't last five minutes in Nathan's Famous July Fourth International Hot Dog Eating Contest. Nathan's Famous July Fourth International Hot Dog Eating Contest reminds me of bullfighting, capitalism and pole dancing.

Summer, 1982

We are now speaking of evenings in New Orleans when the
world was the time it took to ride my bike from Galvez St. to
the French Quarter where I pedaled on the cathedral's
cobblestone to watch tourists wipe powdered sugar from their
lips and, drunk on Bourbon, learn that jazz was molten, beaten
on the anvil of some braless alto until every cigarette was lit.

New Orleans

Sweaty garter easing down
the sax

Striptease in the keys

All the while
Wynton's patois rung

fingered   flung

Travel this highway   traveler you

Be on the lookout for whatever
steadies you

Trumpet   three valves   every color blown

Ovation in peacock
feathered notes

flown

Witnesses

They don't have answers because they say they have answers through the screen door. Yet memories of my momma make me pause for these women whose sistren, 30 years ago, would stand on our front porch knocking. Momma would shush me as we watched them from behind the French shutters in my bedroom. Momma in her house dress, hair long like the women with their unmade faces, bare earlobes, Bibles and *Watchtower*. Momma never said anything bad about them. She just taught me to wait out the truth.

French Quarter

Instead of art
I'll have one boy
from dusk
one boy
who knows the relevance
of his body
Almost no words
will pass between us
until we rinse the hours
from glad bodies
marooned not long enough
for the paradise we took

Without Angels

Was it the horn in his pants
that made it clear
you were a faggot
misspelled by God
kindling for a church
and a mother looking gone
when you told her

What else sent you
to the windowsill

The rake
your leaves
Eternal autumn
stupid in-between

Barnes & Noble

Widening my aperture for Ai
(It's what you want. If you didn't / you wouldn't
beg to be poured into my mouth)
I'm distracted by a young Asian squatting
in front of the philosophy section

Even if I get
that cabin by the creek   patient dog at my feet
while I write my wide poems

I'll think of my car
the road where trains run to the city
the mall near the station
its second-floor bathroom and someone like this man
waiting in a stall
until I get there
to tear down the metal partition
or gently open the door

Uncut

When the clean-shaven one
with the black Porsche asked me
not to clean it
I understood the poetry
in his appetite
whatever would gather until Saturday night
the yellow and white of it
how he'd pull back the skin
one stanza at a time
I'd look away from his trembling fingers
his foraging tongue
and swallow

Armor

Now you got me thinking
about that boy
chain mail
under his robe of hoodie

Damn R!
It's like a concealed revolver
You know there's heat
something giving swagger
Imagine all the broken teeth
between us
how I would actually take
nigger whispered
into each lobe
Fuck nigger   tender
miraculous mending
we could do
this reckless boy
brandishing youth

I'd let him take my wallet

Shit I'd give him the password
to my Facebook account so he could
read my emails and vandalize walls
And if pedigree is a collar
on a leash
let him yank and shorten it
tie it down and go medieval
on my ass

Salvation

Leather boots
two polished exclamations
that he belongs wherever he is
I squint for other memories
of the tall state trooper
whose silence I always matched
But this fills the frame

I raise my father
through leather
ascend tightening bootstraps
summon his silence
through a head harness
a mouth gag pulled tight
hoist a man's whimpers
as sails

Believe me   I know what to console
what to injure and speak holy

Tell me you've never looked at Jesus hanging there
the way you look at any man
before you caught yourself and averted your eyes
from the blunt brutal evidence
that salvation is only possible
when your god is hungry
then fed

Serpent

An apple's hollowed crown
kindling ganja
One small hole on its side
to inhale
One West Indian woman
to shepherd me to the place
smoke clears
a bed for harvesting my phantom limb
in flesh and nerves
to ride its blood and for once
forbid the fruit to ripen
in my own lonely hand
but let it fatten
bloom to the weight of deliciousness
inside this man

If I must be born again
let me enter his womb
his right thumb in my mouth
his legs in the stirrups
of my shouldering

Jesus loves me
this I know
my man's body
tells me so

Clenched

Whenever moved
I'm carefully measured
shake my head instead of sob
brace the arm flying upward to praise
or bite the sudden whip
of my tongue

On a tarmac outside New Orleans
three hours
from my mother who's given up
who won't let the levee water recede
the fluid filling her calves

The Latino next to me expresses interest
but I clench and watch the little girl across the aisle
whose sleeping father doesn't know
she's messed herself

She keeps looking at me crying
for some sign that I would
maybe
take possession of her for a moment
make her clean again

Rent

for Mitchell McCarthy

Any part of this would be hard to tell
Even how I walked his back to ease the tightening
Even the rent-controlled apartment he and Victor shared for years
absurd in Harlem for under a grand
Six big rooms

He'd danced   But there was no controlling his body then
Dance Theatre held a memorial   They'd become routine
But he'd made it to '91
Danced through full blown stages

I saw Victor in *Miss Saigon* in '94   He sang out of tune
Rent is a much better musical but it's hard
to keep track at first   Not just one person is dying
And it's so emotionally draining since they're all young
and not supposed to die yet

The music's awful but the story rightfully complicated
torn

Elegy for Castrati

for Alessandro Moreschi and all his brothers

Priests or their henchmen went for the boys
drew a hot bath till they fainted
Glissando to flesh
Gory to God

Petitions & scales for succulent song
Lord mercy
Christ mercy
Laud to fell the boys

Others lost their bleak soprano
Gorged coffered spirits sacked
on they swaggered
tenor bass

Faces flat hairless huge
boy castrati stayed
Vaulted throats flayed the praise
Organs utterly raged

Golden pipes shot homeward
pulleys of screeching praise
singed the heels of seraphim
Organs utterly crazed

A mass of pulp to masturbate
behind the harpsichord
orchestral body fingered heft
left as its own reward

The Man without Eyes in Kuala Lumpur

I saw your hands first

Wondrous beggar I thought
Those two candles that sit in the face
to burn in unison were in unison
unlit and I passed from them into prayer
stumbling into the street   making a u-turn
to see how you didn't see
and to place five ringgits as gently as I could
into your smiling hands

I stood in the street zoomed to the limit
The shutter blinked
Other mourners asked why
with their eyes

You were there the next day
a fixture like any other so I took
another picture
You'll go to hell for this
I said to myself

If I make it into heaven
you'll be most familiar
Our bodies will have been left
you   with less
to leave

Typhoid Mary

Irish wonder cook
wondered why
the tick and lot of you
was lethal
To be told that
you know

Wondered woman
sat down before your blood
and begged it
Turn

Thirty years on Brother Island
eating hosts round and changed
Ah Mary
named so inappropriately

We hear your magnificat
just above the hard rule
of stool and piss

The Truth, Nothing But

for Elvis

Little Richard was angry for years
He'd given up the Gospel
to somebody white and pretty
who kept begging in that sexy drawl
heavier
than a roll of quarters

Show me how to turn my bones
to brown sugar
I wanna be sweet
I wanna be sweet

Witness

*after the concert by Marian Anderson sponsored by the
Phillis Wheatley Literary Club, Charleston, 1926*

We rode your voice through Handel and Debussy
our backs straight

The sun-swallowing bloom of your soprano
measured and wild

Your hand on the piano
you in its curve

As the spirituals washed down

Sometimes I feel like a motherless child
Dere's no hidin' place down dere

Monday night became Sunday morning
and you had a choir Marian

You had a brand new choir

KEVIN SIMMONDS is a writer, musician and performance artist originally from New Orleans. He edited *Collective Brightness: LGBTIQ Poets on Faith, Religion & Spirituality* (Sibling Rivalry Press) and *Ota Benga Under My Mother's Roof* (University of South Carolina Press), a collection of poetry by the late poet and writer Carrie Allen McCray-Nickens. He wrote the music for *Wisteria: Twilight Songs from the Swamp Country*, a performance collaboration with poet Kwame Dawes that made its European debut at the Poetry International Festival at London's Royal Festival Hall and was the subject of a BBC documentary. He also wrote the music for the Emmy Award-winning documentary *HOPE: Living and Loving with HIV in Jamaica*. He has received awards, fellowships and residencies from Atlantic Center for the Arts, Cave Canem Foundation, Fulbright, Jack Straw and San Francisco Arts Commission. He received the Bachelor of Music at Vanderbilt University and the PhD in music at the University of South Carolina. He divides his time between Japan and San Francisco. *Mad for Meat* is his first collection of poetry.